TECH BYTES
EXPLORING SPACE

THE INTERNATIONAL SPACE STATION

BY JOYCE MARKOVICS

NORWOOD HOUSE PRESS

NORWOOD HOUSE PRESS

Cover: A view of the International Space Station (ISS) from space.

For more information about Norwood House Press, please visit our website at: www.norwoodhousepress.com or call 866-565-2900.

Book Designer: Ed Morgan
Editorial and Production: Bowerbird Books
Content Consultant: Dr. Joel Green, Astrophysicist

Photo Credits: freepik.com, cover and title page; NASA/Norah Moran, 4; freepik.com, 5; freepik.com, 6; NASA, 7; NASA, 8–9; NASA, 10; NASA, 11; NASA, 12; NASA, 13; NASA, 14; NASA, 15; NASA, 16; NASA, 17; NASA, 18; NASA/Robert Markowitz, 19; NASA, 21; NASA, 22; NASA, 23; NASA, 24; NASA/Scott Kelly, 25; NASA, 26; NASA, 27; NASA, 28; NASA, 29; NASA, 30–31; NASA, 32; NASA, 33; NASA, 34; NASA, 35; NASA/Boeing, 36–37; Public Domain/Axiom Space Inc., 38; Public Domain/Axiom Space Inc., 39; NASA, 40; NASA, 41; NASA/Bill Ingalls, 42; NASA, 43.

Copyright © 2023 Norwood House Press

Hardcover ISBN: 978-1-68450-727-6
Paperback ISBN: 978-1-68404-839-7

All rights reserved. No part of this book may be reproduced or utilized in any form or by any means without written permission from the publisher.

Library of Congress Cataloging-in-Publication Data

Names: Markovics, Joyce L., author.
Title: The International Space Station / by Joyce Markovics.
Description: [Chicago] : Norwood House Press, [2023] | Series: Tech bytes : exploring space | Includes bibliographical references and index. | Audience: Grades 4-6
Identifiers: LCCN 2022038804 (print) | LCCN 2022038805 (ebook) | ISBN 9781684507276 (hardcover) | ISBN 9781684048397 (paperback) | ISBN 9781684048595 (ebook)
Subjects: LCSH: International Space Station--Juvenile literature. | Space stations--Juvenile literature. | Life support systems (Space environment)--Juvenile literature.
Classification: LCC TL797.15 .M27 2023 (print) | LCC TL797.15 (ebook) | DDC 629.44/2--dc23/eng/20221003
LC record available at https://lccn.loc.gov/2022038804
LC ebook record available at https://lccn.loc.gov/2022038805

359N—012023

Manufactured in the United States of America in North Mankato, Minnesota.

CONTENTS

CHAPTER 1
Space Mission.................... 4

CHAPTER 2
Building the ISS................... 10

CHAPTER 3
Life on the Station................. 20

CHAPTER 4
The Future of the ISS............. 36

Glossary — 44
For More Information — 46
Index — 48
About the Author — 48

Words that are bolded in the text are defined in the glossary.

CHAPTER 1
SPACE MISSION

At 7:27 PM on November 16, 2020, **NASA astronauts** Mike Hopkins, Victor Glover, and Shannon Walker blasted off on an incredible trip. They were joined by Japanese Space Agency (JAXA) astronaut Soichi Noguchi. Traveling aboard a SpaceX capsule attached to a rocket, they left Kennedy Space Center in Florida on a space mission. Technology made every step of their journey possible. The astronauts squeezed inside the SpaceX capsule, which is about as roomy as the inside of a small van. As their spacecraft shot into the **atmosphere** over the Atlantic Ocean, it lit up the night sky.

Pictured from left to right are astronauts Shannon Walker, Victor Glover, Mike Hopkins, and Soichi Noguchi.

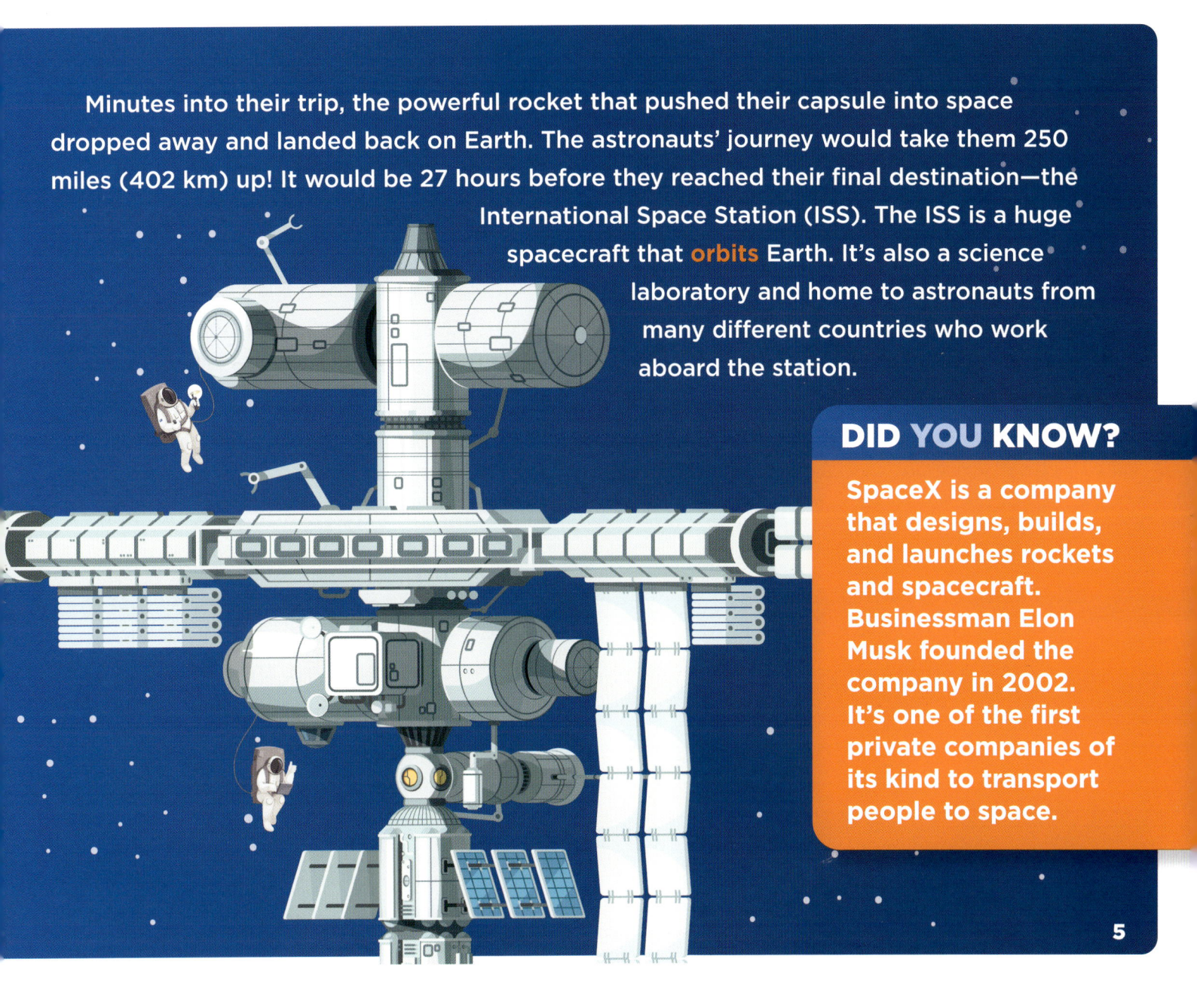

Minutes into their trip, the powerful rocket that pushed their capsule into space dropped away and landed back on Earth. The astronauts' journey would take them 250 miles (402 km) up! It would be 27 hours before they reached their final destination—the International Space Station (ISS). The ISS is a huge spacecraft that orbits Earth. It's also a science laboratory and home to astronauts from many different countries who work aboard the station.

DID YOU KNOW?

SpaceX is a company that designs, builds, and launches rockets and spacecraft. Businessman Elon Musk founded the company in 2002. It's one of the first private companies of its kind to transport people to space.

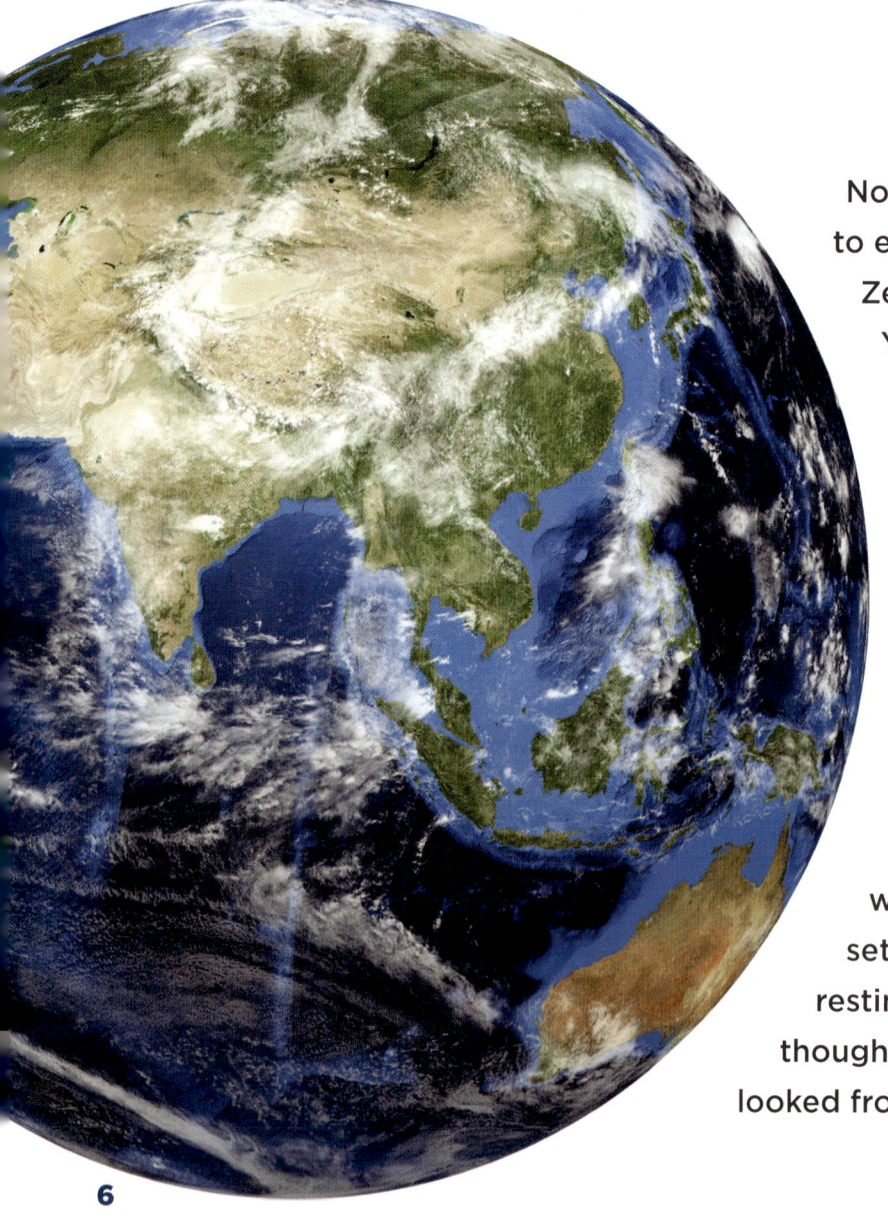

Not long after liftoff, the astronauts began to experience what's called zero gravity, or Zero-G. They knew this when the Baby Yoda stuffed animal they brought with them began to float inside the capsule! The crew members also felt themselves floating out of their seats. About an hour into the ride, Mike Hopkins used digital technology to communicate with the NASA crew on the ground: "That was one heck of a ride." He also shared how happy the astronauts were, especially Victor Glover, the youngest crew member. It was his first spaceflight. The crew then settled in for a long trip, taking turns resting and glancing down at Earth. They thought about how beautiful the planet looked from space.

IS THERE GRAVITY IN SPACE?

Gravity is the force on Earth that holds you to the ground. For example, when you jump up in the air, gravity is what causes you to come back down. However, in space, astronauts and other things appear to float. In fact, there is a small amount of gravity in space. It's called microgravity. Because the astronauts are so far from Earth, the strength of gravity they feel is much weaker than on the ground. Because microgravity is not very strong, it makes things seem weightless. But the truth is the astronauts are in free fall. Have you ever been on a roller coaster when it races down a big hill? Did you feel yourself lifting out of your seat? Then you experienced free fall. The same thing happens to people and objects in space.

An astronaut watches her tortilla and a jar float inside a space shuttle.

WELCOME ABOARD

After a long trip, the SpaceX capsule arrived at the ISS. Catching up to the space station wasn't easy. Why? It's traveling at 17,000 miles (27,359 km) per hour! The ISS travels all the way around Earth every hour and a half. Once the capsule neared the station, its onboard computer helped it steer to a special dock. Then the capsule automatically connected it to the dock and space station. Finally, the astronauts were able to open the hatch on the capsule and safely enter the ISS. They were there to begin a six-month-long mission.

The crew was greeted by three other astronauts already living on the ISS. After catching up, the tired travelers went to sleep. It had been a long trip, and they needed to prepare for their mission on the ISS. Each day would be packed with activities, including science experiments, performing maintenance on the station, and squeezing in time to connect with their families back on Earth.

The SpaceX capsule docked at the International Space Station about 264 miles (425 km) above southern Brazil.

CHAPTER 2
BUILDING the ISS

Construction of the International Space Station began in 1998. The ISS would be so huge that it could not be launched into space on a single rocket. Instead, it would be built in pieces, and each piece would be launched into space. Several countries, including the United States, Russia, Japan, and many countries in Europe, worked together and shared their best technology to build parts of the station. Russian scientists built and launched a module called Zarya. A module is like an enormous tube—similar to the pressurized cabin of an airplane. About 41 feet (12 m) long and 13 feet (4 m) wide, Zarya was the first **component** of the ISS. Zarya would provide power, storage, and **propulsion** to the station.

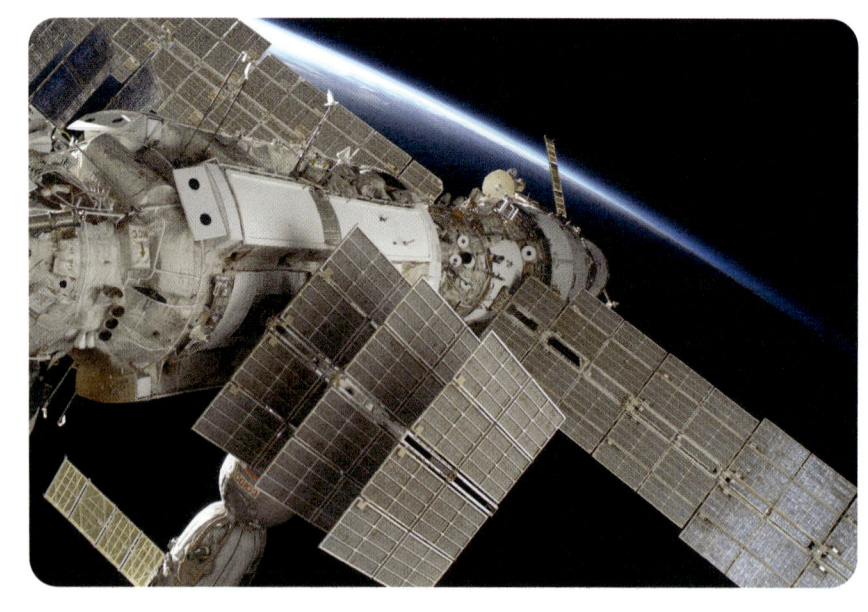

The Russian word *Zarya* means "sunrise" in English.

Unity (in the distance) flies toward Zarya.

Then the United States built another component called Unity, which is known as a connecting node. It would be the first of three nodes. A shuttle carried Unity to space where NASA astronaut Nancy Currie used a robotic arm to join it with the Zarya module. This was no easy task. The lead flight director said it was "the most difficult mission the shuttle has ever had to fly." But the NASA team also knew there would be more complicated missions ahead in order to fully assemble the ISS.

DID YOU KNOW?

Unity and the other nodes contain more than 50,000 smaller parts and hundreds of lines and cables that carry fluids, gases, and electricity throughout the ISS.

The interior of the Zvezda module

In 2000, Russia built and sent another module, called Zvezda, to the growing ISS. Zvezda would allow for astronauts to live onboard and control the space station, as well as communicate with **colleagues** on Earth. That same year, Russian astronauts—known as cosmonauts—and one American astronaut traveled to the ISS to live there, work on the station, and start conducting experiments.

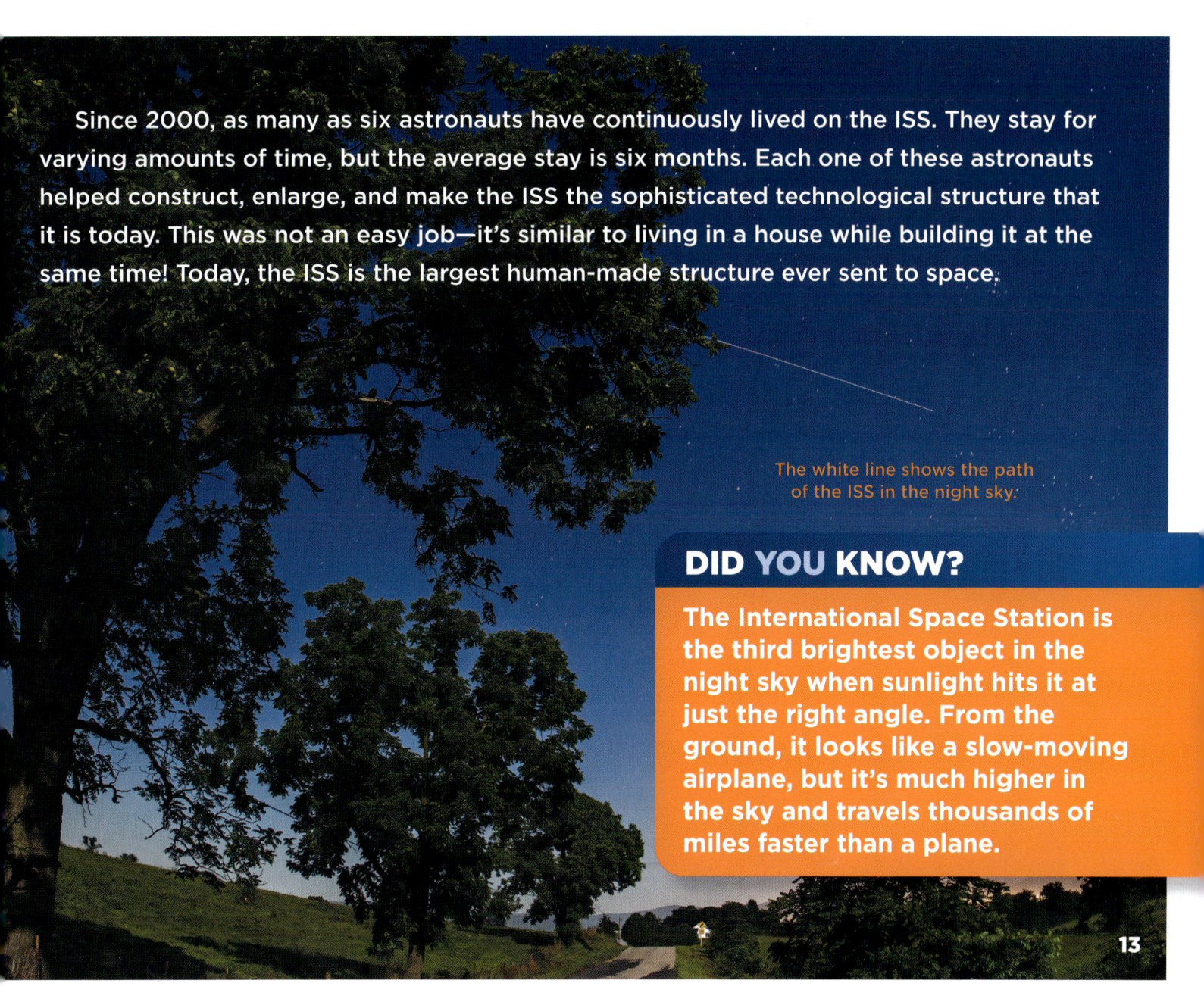

Since 2000, as many as six astronauts have continuously lived on the ISS. They stay for varying amounts of time, but the average stay is six months. Each one of these astronauts helped construct, enlarge, and make the ISS the sophisticated technological structure that it is today. This was not an easy job—it's similar to living in a house while building it at the same time! Today, the ISS is the largest human-made structure ever sent to space.

The white line shows the path of the ISS in the night sky.

DID YOU KNOW?

The International Space Station is the third brightest object in the night sky when sunlight hits it at just the right angle. From the ground, it looks like a slow-moving airplane, but it's much higher in the sky and travels thousands of miles faster than a plane.

PARTS of the ISS

For many years, space shuttles have carried modules, supplies, and maintenance crews to the ISS. It has taken decades to put together all the parts. The ISS is known as a modular station because it is built from various modules. Each module can be removed or added as necessary. The other major parts of the International Space Station include an enormous **truss** structure—made from many smaller metal triangles—that forms the backbone of the station. The trusses help support one of the most noticeable parts of the space station—its huge, rectangular solar arrays. Solar arrays are used to harness the Sun's energy to make power.

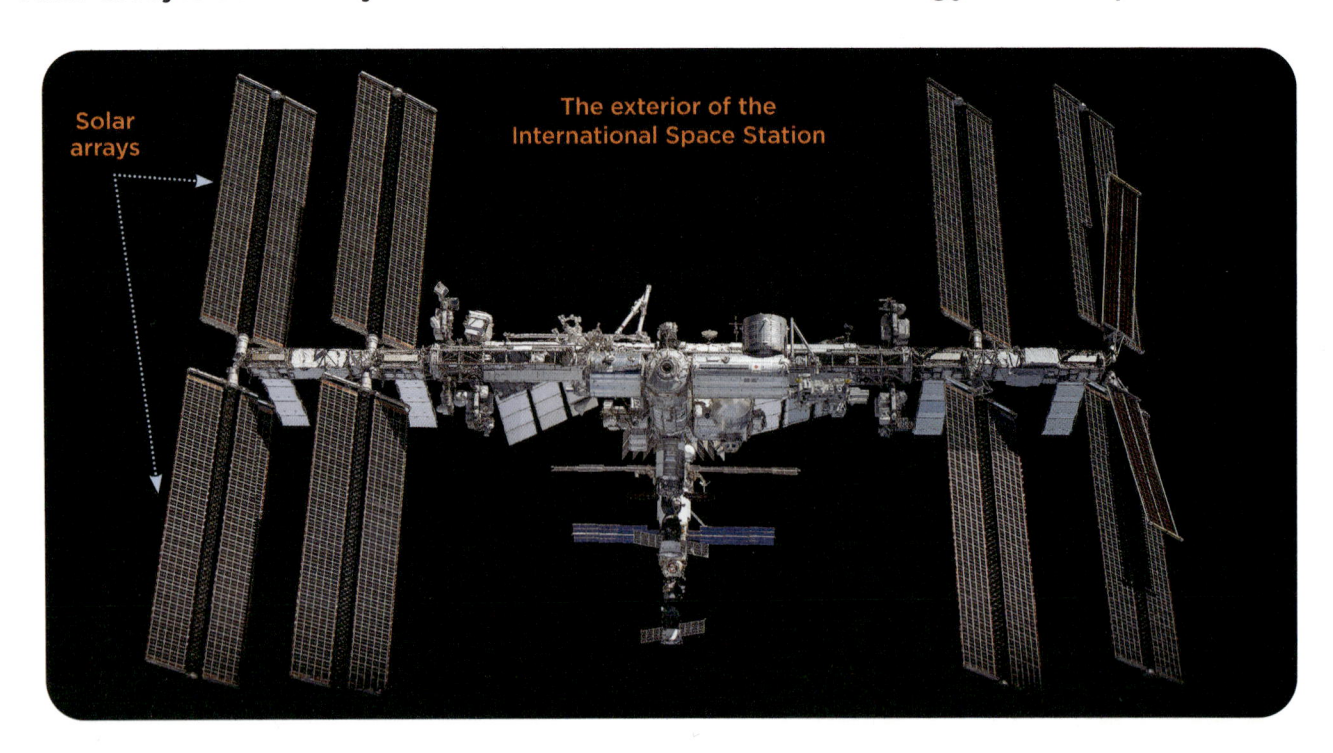

Solar arrays

The exterior of the International Space Station

SOLAR ARRAYS

The ISS's winglike solar arrays are covered with photovoltaic, or solar, cells that are made from thin slices of silicon. Silicon is a semiconductor. When exposed to the Sun's light, a semiconductor produces an electric current. NASA figured out a way to mount the solar cells on a "blanket" that can be rolled up, transported, and easily mounted. After being installed, the solar arrays are programmed to face the Sun. That way, they can take in the maximum amount of the Sun's energy to power the station. Together, the arrays can generate enough electricity to power 40 homes on Earth.

A close-up view of the ISS's solar arrays

15

The ISS's trusses also provide support to **thermal** radiators, another important technological component of the station. The thermal radiators are waffle-shaped panels that help get rid of extra heat that builds up in the station. Energy from the solar arrays flows into the station's electrical systems, all of which produce heat. Without radiators to **dissipate** this heat, the station would become extremely hot and uninhabitable for humans. "The excess heat is removed by this very efficient liquid heat-exchange system," says Gene Ungar, a thermal specialist at NASA. Then the heat energy goes to the radiators and is released into space.

Construction of the truss structure over New Zealand

Insulation is another critical part of the station. The outside of the ISS is wrapped in layers of different materials that protect the station from the Sun's heat, extreme cold, and space **debris**. These materials include shiny aluminum, **Kevlar**, and heat-resistant ceramics. Except for the windows, the entire space station is covered with this special insulation.

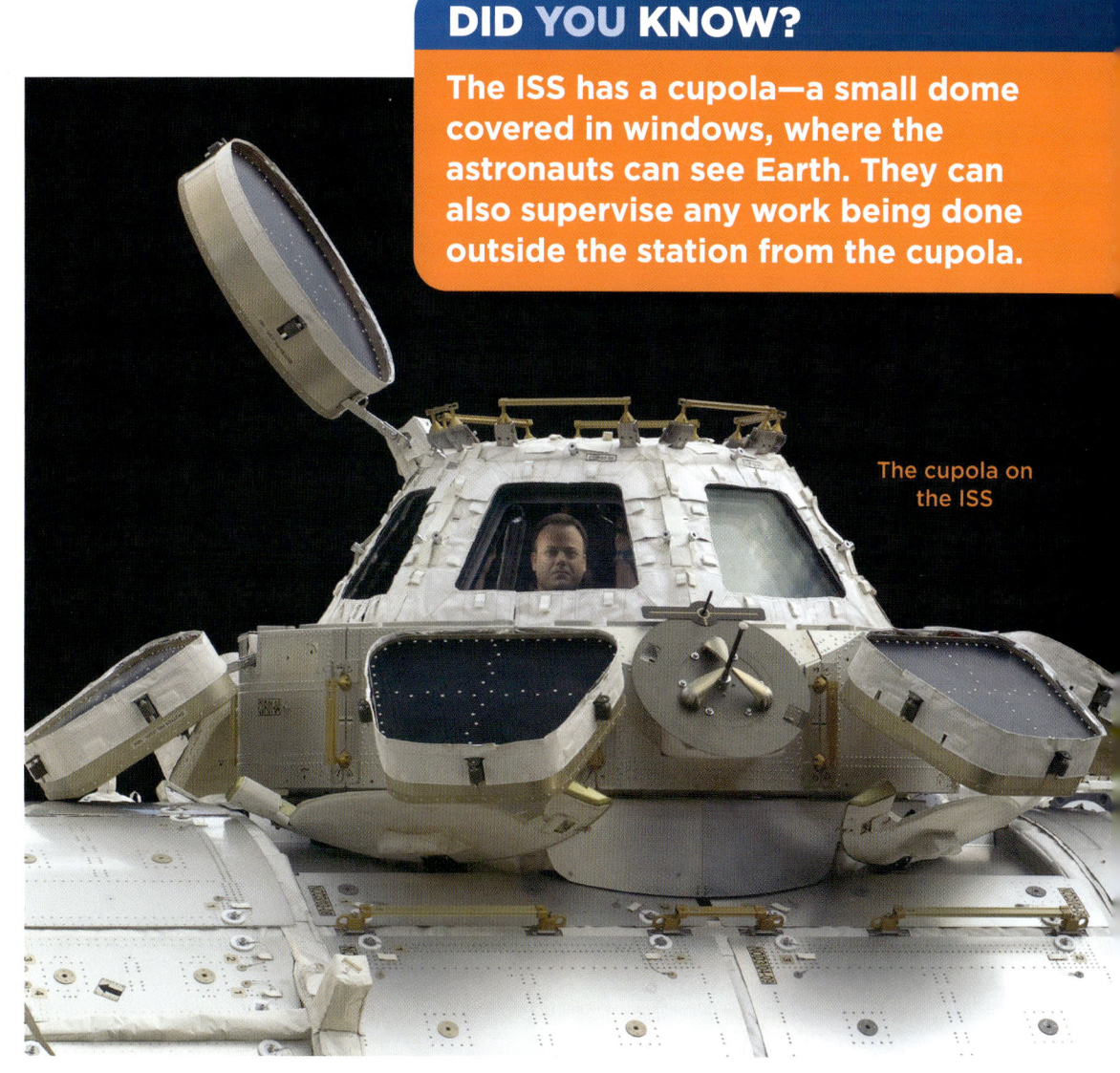

DID YOU KNOW?

The ISS has a cupola—a small dome covered in windows, where the astronauts can see Earth. They can also supervise any work being done outside the station from the cupola.

The cupola on the ISS

The ISS's robotic arm is known as Canadarm2. It was created by scientists and engineers at the Canadian Space Agency (CSA).

Dextre

And
ROBOTS
TOO!

The International Space Station also uses technology with an extra-long reach. The station has a giant robotic arm connected to its middle section. The arm is big and strong enough to move modules and multiple astronauts, yet it can also perform more delicate tasks, especially with the help of Dextre. This robotic handyman is able to ride on the end of the robotic arm called Canadarm2. It can perform some routine repairs and other jobs so the astronauts don't have to. This keeps the astronauts safe inside the ISS and gives them more time to conduct experiments.

ISS MISSION CONTROL

The ISS is not just controlled by the astronauts and technological systems onboard. The ISS has mission controls across Earth. From the ground, flight control teams monitor the space station every minute of every day. From the Johnson Space Center in Texas, they watch the crew to keep them safe and healthy and check on the spacecraft systems to ensure everything is running as it should. The flight controllers are also prepared should something go wrong, such as a malfunctioning robotic arm or computer.

Mission Control Central at NASA's Johnson Space Center

CHAPTER 3
LIFE on the STATION

Inside, the ISS is bustling with life. The station has served as the location of more than 2,400 experiments and investigations. The ISS is the best place to test the effects of weightlessness and microgravity on living things. This is the kind of work Mike Hopkins, Victor Glover, and Shannon Walker began after they arrived on the space station in November 2020.

Every day is different for astronauts on the space station. When Shannon Walker wakes up on the ISS, the first thing she does is check her schedule for the day. "Usually, we have some activities that can be done at any time and some that have to be done on the timeline as scheduled," said Shannon. After figuring out her schedule, she checks in with control centers on Earth. Several cities around the world have control centers that help the ISS operate and manage the science experiments conducted onboard. This is important because the ISS goes all the way around Earth every 90 minutes, so to stay in contact, the astronauts have to communicate with different stations across Earth at different times.

DID YOU KNOW?
NASA contributed a microgravity laboratory called Destiny to the station, as well as other labs and habitats.

ASTRONAUT VICTOR GLOVER

Victor "Ike" Glover grew up in Pomona, California. He played football in high school and studied engineering in college. He became an astronaut in 2013. Victor made history when he became the first Black astronaut to be a member of the ISS crew. When asked how he felt about his accomplishment, Victor said, "I am honored to be in this position and to be a part of this great and experienced crew." Victor went on to say, "It will take all of us exploring, learning, and building together to create a brighter future for humanity."

Victor floats inside the ISS.

The next thing that Shannon and the other astronauts do to start their day is exercise. Exercise is extremely important for people living in space. Shannon and the other astronauts spend about two hours each day working out. Why? Microgravity can have some serious effects on the human body. One of the biggest problems is the loss of bone and muscle mass. This happens in a "weightless" environment because bones no longer have to support the body against the pull of gravity.

Exercising in space

To counteract the effects of microgravity on the body, the astronauts use technology in the form of different exercise machines to stay healthy and strong. There's a special kind of weight machine that uses **resistance** instead of actual weights, a treadmill that the astronauts attach themselves to with bungee cords so they don't float away, and an exercise bike. "Because we're in space, we don't need to sit down when we use the bike, so there's no seat," said Victor.

CEVIS, the ISS's exercise bike

DID YOU KNOW?

The ISS's exercise bike is called CEVIS. That's short for Cycle Ergometer with Vibration Isolation System. It's bolted to the floor, and astronauts attach their shoes to the pedals. Then a seat belt holds them down while they're pedaling!

23

LABORATORIES and EXPERIMENTS

After exercising, it's time for more work. Shannon and the other astronauts are involved in a variety of different experiments, which can vary from testing a new system to remove heat from spacesuits to analyzing living tissue. One such experiment involved testing small pieces of tissue that were similar to larger human organs. This was done in order to understand how microgravity affects the human body and diseased body parts. The astronauts also tended plants growing inside an area on the ISS devoted to space **botany**.

Growing plants in space is key to ensuring that astronauts stay healthy during long missions. Vitamin **deficiencies** can cause a multitude of health issues, and multivitamins are not enough to solve the problem. Also, over time, the vitamins in the prepackaged foods that astronauts eat break down. Fresh vegetables, fruit, and other produce are needed to keep astronauts from getting sick. Yet how are plants grown in a spacecraft with little sunlight and gravity?

Kale and other leafy greens grown in the ISS

SPACE BOUQUET

Scientists are interested in more than just growing vegetables in space. They're also investigating ways to grow fresh flowers. Flowers are a way of bringing a small but beautiful part of Earth to space. They're also good for mental health. On an earlier mission, astronaut Scott Kelly grew colorful zinnia flowers, which he made into a bouquet and photographed in the cupola against the backdrop of Earth. He shared the photo on Valentine's Day.

Zinnia flowers grown in space

The astronauts tended a space garden on the ISS known as the Vegetable Production System, or simply Veggie. The garden is compact, only about the size of a large suitcase, and holds several plants. Each plant grows in what looks like a small pillow that's filled with soil and **fertilizer**. The pillows maintain the right balance of water, nutrients, soil, and air around the plants' roots. Above the garden are LED (light emitting **diodes**) lights that give the plants the ideal **spectrum** of light they need to grow.

Crops growing in space

DID YOU KNOW?

Veggies grown using the ISS's Vegetable Production System include different types of lettuces, Chinese cabbage, red Russian kale, and mizuna mustard.

Here an astronaut cares for different kinds of lettuces aboard the ISS.

Astronauts also used the Advanced Plant Habitat, or APH, which is an **automated** chamber, to grow plants to study. They grew radishes using different types of light and soil. The APH has cameras and more than 180 sensors that monitor every aspect of the plants. The astronauts gathered samples of the plants to send to Earth for testing so scientists can better understand how plant growth is affected by space.

SPACEWALKS

In addition to conducting experiments, astronauts must also work to maintain and repair the ISS. One of the most dangerous jobs is the spacewalk or EVA (extra-vehicular activity). While stationed at the ISS, Mike Hopkins and Victor Glover conducted several spacewalks. One took place on March 13, 2021, and lasted close to seven hours! Their goal was to improve the station's communications and cooling systems. They started their mission by floating into the Quest airlock. This airtight room has two entrances that allow astronauts to go on spacewalks without letting air out of the station. After powering up their suits, Mike and Victor exited the airlock. They traveled to a solar power truss where they completed their first task—venting ammonia, a part of the ISS's cooling system.

An astronaut in the Quest airlock

SPACESUIT BASICS

There are two main types of spacesuits. One is worn inside a spacecraft when an astronaut is traveling to space. The other is designed specifically for spacewalks. This high-tech suit is like a tiny wearable spaceship that protects the astronaut from the dangers of space. These dangers include radiation, dust, debris, and extremely cold or hot temperatures. The spacesuit also provides an astronaut with just the right pressure, oxygen to breathe, and water to drink.

Victor Glover is pictured during a spacewalk to service the station's cooling system and communications gear.

Then the two astronauts tackled parts of the communications system, which proved more challenging. After a few hours, they joked about popping into the ISS for some "snacks and bacon"! Most astronauts agree that spacewalks are one of the most demanding jobs—both physically and mentally—they must complete in space. Every 90 minutes, the astronauts go through cycles of day and night and hot and cold as the ISS whizzes around Earth at 17,000 miles (27,359 km) per hour. This speed is how the ISS stays in orbit above Earth as it balances out the pull of Earth's gravity. Mike was only able to get three out of four cables in place. Mission control watched his every move and assisted him as needed.

Michael Hopkins is pictured during a spacewalk servicing communications gear on the outside of the International Space Station's Columbus laboratory module.

DID YOU KNOW?

Close to 250 spacewalks have taken place at the ISS since construction began in 1998.

Affixed to Mike's helmet was a **high-definition** camera that recorded every minute of his spacewalk. Finally, after connecting the last cable, Mike jokingly said, "And the crowd goes wild!" The astronauts also reconfigured a radio antenna and routed two **Ethernet** cables that would expand the ISS's **Wi-Fi** network. Their spacewalk was considered a great success.

SLEEPING in SPACE

After a long day of spacewalks and experiments, astronauts need rest. Sleeping on the International Space Station is not at all like sleeping on Earth. Bedrooms are about the size of phone booths. Because there's no real up or down, astronauts can sleep in any direction they're comfortable. Astronauts climb inside sleeping bags secured to the walls so they don't float away. Even when they're asleep, astronauts are using technology. They wear devices that monitor and record how well they're sleeping, their vital signs, and more.

An astronaut tucked into a sleeping bag in a bedroom on the ISS

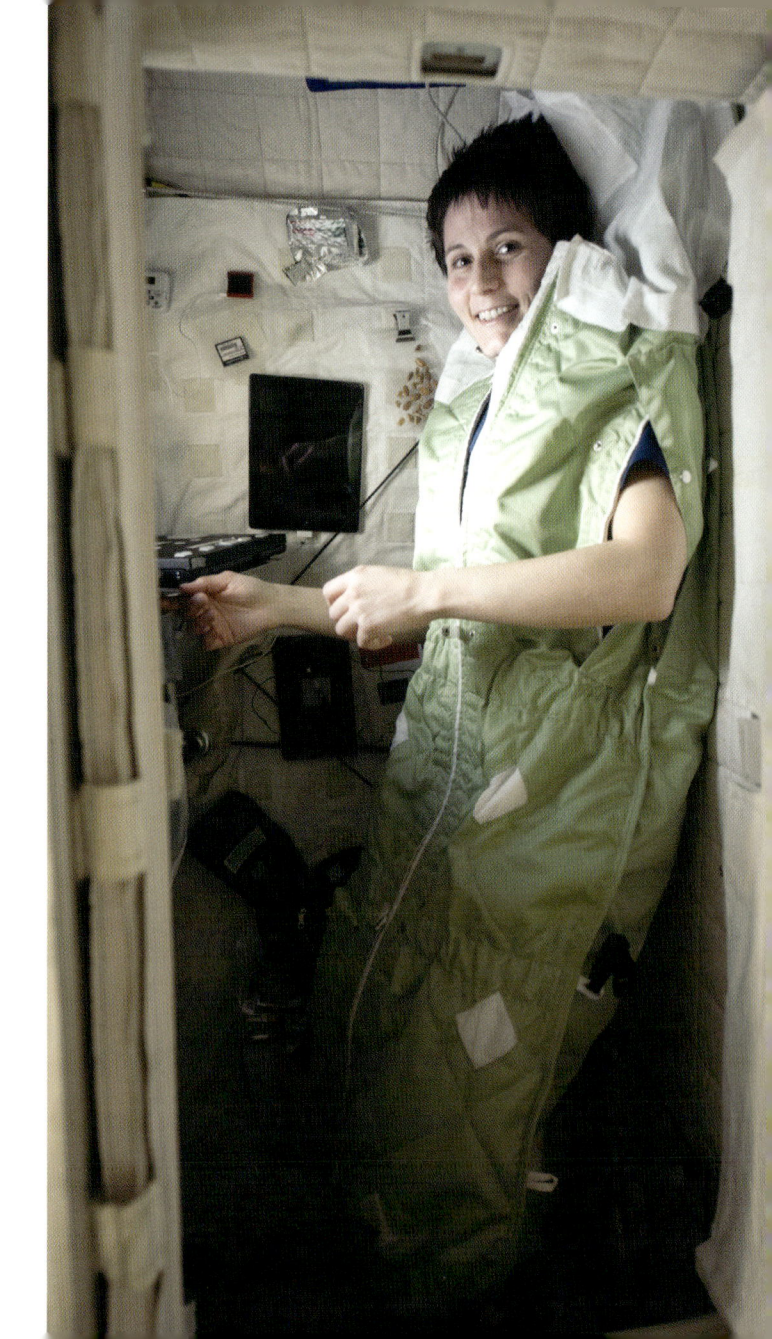

GOT TO GO! SPACE TOILET

On the International Space Station, technology helps people use the bathroom! There is a container that collects solid waste. There's a separate hose that collects urine. A machine recycles urine and turns it into fresh water! In space, every drop of water is precious. "We recycle about 90 percent of all water-based liquids on the space station, including urine and sweat," explains NASA astronaut Jessica Meir. "What we try to do aboard the space station is mimic elements of Earth's natural water cycle to reclaim water from the air. And when it comes to our urine on ISS, today's coffee is tomorrow's coffee!"

This is what a bathroom looks like on the ISS. To prevent stuff from floating away, everything is strapped down.

This astronaut conducts an eye exam on herself.

Vital signs include a person's pulse, temperature, breathing, and blood pressure. The wearable devices can also detect stress. Together, the data from this technology can indicate an astronaut's health. The special devices also send information to scientists on Earth, who keep track of the astronauts' day-to-day health. The goal is for the astronauts to stay as healthy and strong as possible in space.

Thanks to the devices, scientists also learn about the short- and long-term effects of microgravity on the body. For instance, living in microgravity can cause fluid to build up in the head. This can change the shape of an astronaut's eyeballs, leading to vision problems. A private company has invented a high-tech sleeping bag that pushes body fluids from the head to the lower body, preventing space-related eye issues. After a good night's rest, astronauts are ready to begin a new day of work. Thanks to technology aboard the ISS, they're able to do so healthily and safely.

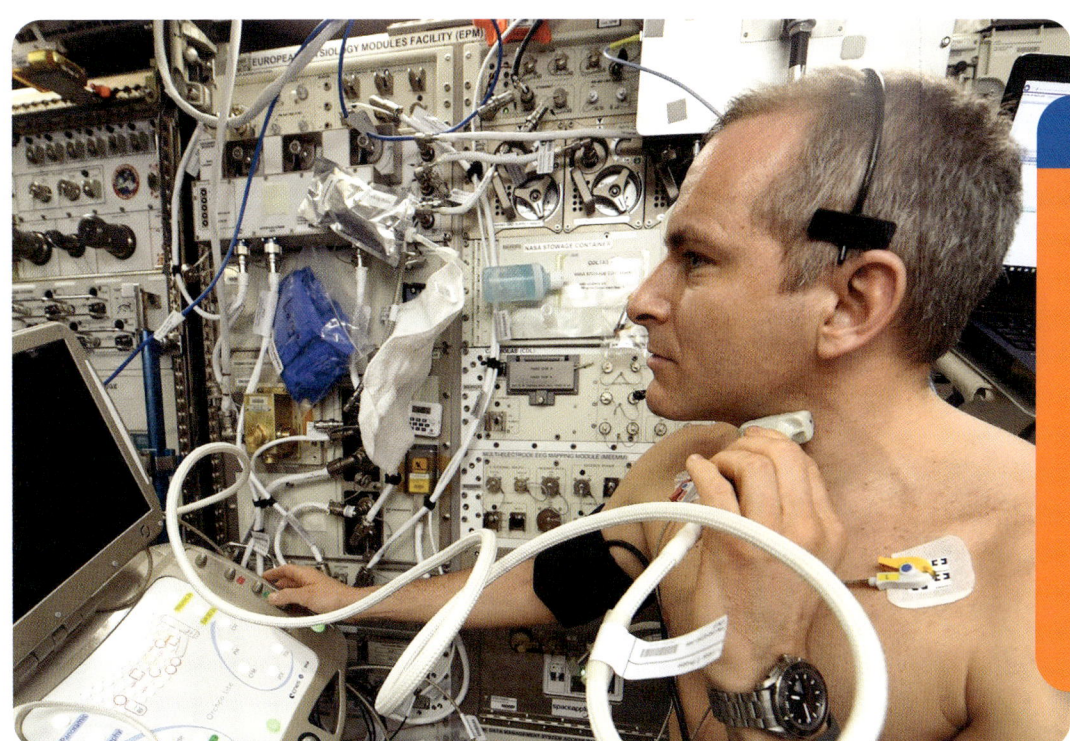

Another astronaut monitors his heart health.

DID YOU KNOW?

Microgravity has an effect on the human heart as well. It pulls blood from the heart and changes its shape from an oval—like a water balloon—to a rounder baseball shape. This causes the heart to work less efficiently.

CHAPTER 4
The FUTURE of the ISS

Since the ISS was first launched and assembled in space, it has been home to more than 200 astronauts from 19 countries. These astronauts have conducted countless experiments to learn to better live in and explore space. However, the space station is getting old. NASA plans on **decommissioning** it in 2031. So what will happen to it? Without occasional boosting, the space station would eventually fall back to Earth. For our safety, NASA wants to control where it will fall. The agency will bring the football-field-sized spacecraft down into the Pacific Ocean. There's a special place in the ocean near New Zealand called Point Nemo, also known as the "Spacecraft Cemetery." It's where space agencies have sunk more than 250 pieces of space junk.

Smaller space debris often burns up when it reenters the atmosphere. The smaller the space junk, the more easily it burns up on reentry. However, larger space junk needs to be carefully disposed of where it can't harm people. So scientists selected an area of the Pacific Ocean far away from land where **satellites**, spacecraft carrying waste from the ISS including astronaut poop, and old space stations can safely sink to the ocean floor. It's hard not to wonder if the space junk is now home to many deep-sea ocean creatures!

The ISS will one day be in the depths of the Pacific Ocean.

Before the ISS is sunk to the ocean floor, NASA is trying to find private companies like Blue Origin, Sierra Space, and Axiom Space of Houston to help build future space stations. Axiom has already agreed to build a module that it will attach to the ISS around 2024. Axiom and other private companies are working on plans for brand-new space stations. They're using cutting-edge technology to design and build them. The Axiom station will include high-speed Wi-Fi, video screens, picture windows, and a glass cupola.

An illustration of the Axiom module's cupola

This is the design for the Axiom module.

NASA would then pay Axiom and other companies for its astronauts to use these new space stations. "We look forward to sharing our lessons learned and operations experience with the private sector to help them develop safe, reliable, and cost-effective destinations in space," said representatives from NASA.

DID YOU KNOW?

Axiom is run by a former NASA employee who used to be the program manager for the International Space Station.

WHAT'S NEXT for the ISS?

Before the space station is decommissioned, it will be a hive of activity, including research and technology development. There are plans for astronauts from all around the globe to keep traveling and working there. They will continue the important scientific research started by astronauts before them. Future work includes carrying out new experiments, involving studies about **Alzheimer's disease** and portable **ultrasound** machines.

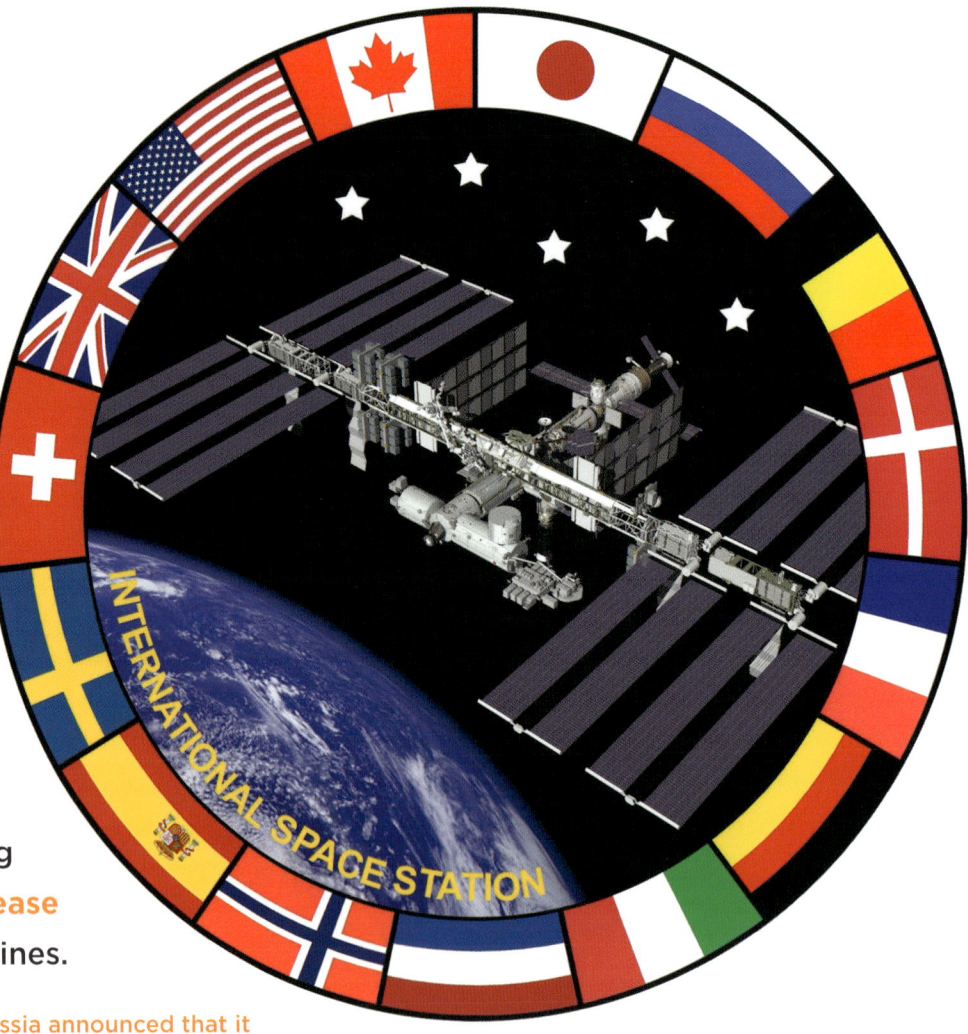

In July 2022, Russia announced that it would leave the ISS after 2024 to focus on building its own space station.

40

Research will also be carried out on the ISS that will help people travel into deep space—and perhaps Mars—in the not-so-distant future. NASA predicts that a human mission to Mars could happen as early as the 2030s thanks to new developments in technology. These include more powerful propulsion systems, high-tech spacesuits, **rovers**, and laser communications to send more information to Earth faster than ever before.

DID YOU KNOW?

A round-trip mission to Mars, also called the Red Planet because of the color of its surface, will take about two years.

This illustration shows what new Mars technology might look like.

RETURN to EARTH

After 167 days in space, Mike, Victor, Shannon, and Soichi returned to Earth. They safely splashed down with the help of several large parachutes into the Gulf of Mexico. They set a record for the longest time in space by a crew that traveled on an American-built spacecraft. The astronauts were plucked out of the ocean by a special recovery ship and then flown back to Houston, Texas, where they were greeted by their families.

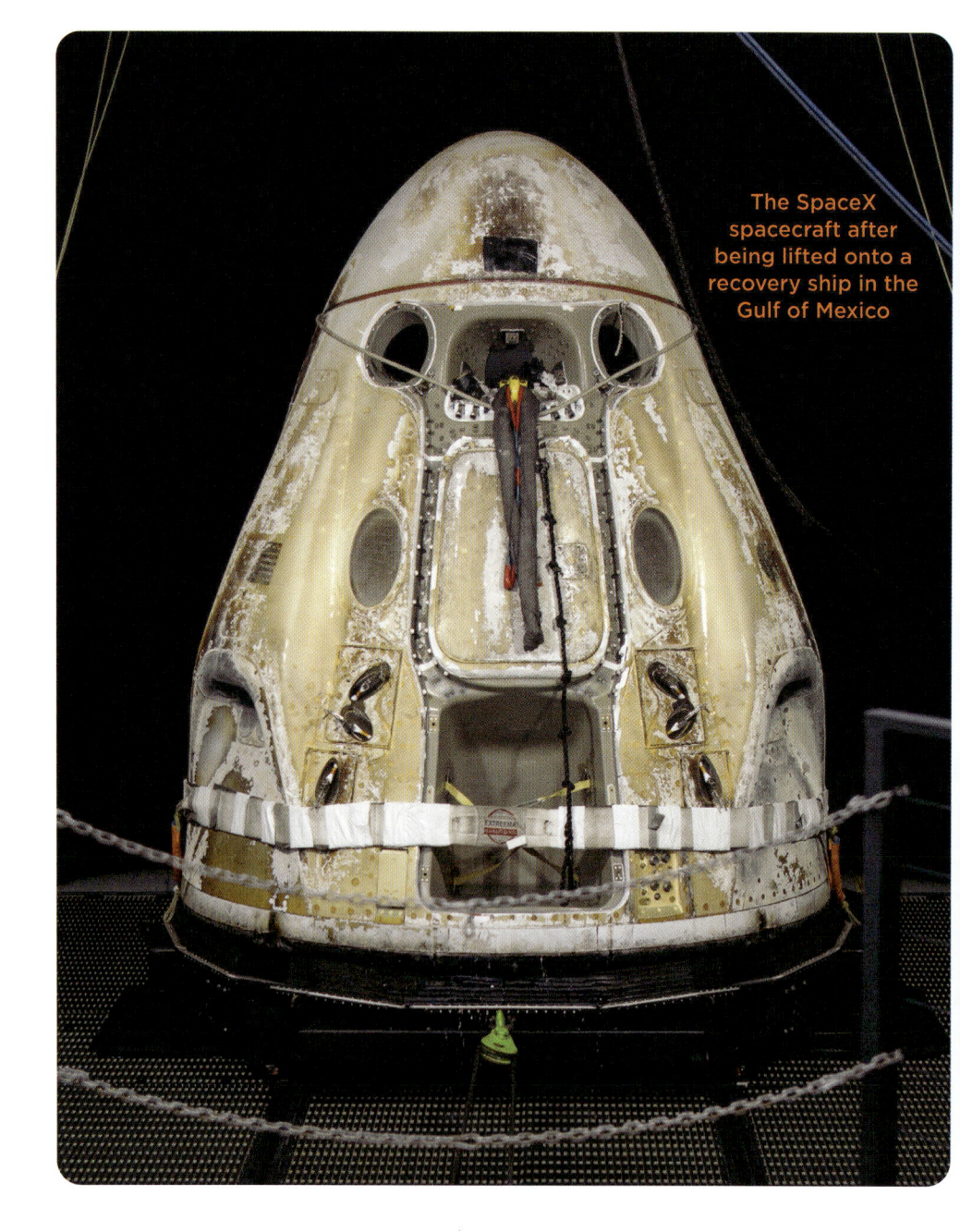

The SpaceX spacecraft after being lifted onto a recovery ship in the Gulf of Mexico

The astronauts safely back on Earth

After returning home, Victor spoke about how moved he was when he saw Earth from space. He said, "I will never forget this moment. . . . It wasn't about the view. It was how the view made me feel . . . the Earth is amazing. It's beautiful. It protects us, and so we should work hard to protect it."

DID YOU KNOW?

The recovery ship has a medical treatment area, helipad, and lifting frame to hoist the SpaceX capsule out of the water.

GLOSSARY

Alzheimer's disease (ALTS-hy-mers dih-ZEEZ): a brain disease that affects the memory that can occur in middle or old age.

astronauts (ASS-truh-nawts): people who travel into space.

atmosphere (AT-muhss-fihr): the mixture of gases surrounding Earth.

automated (AW-tuh-meyt-uhd): operated by equipment that works with little human control.

botany (BOT-n-ee): the science of plants.

colleagues (KOL-eegz): fellow workers.

component (kuhm-POH-huhnt): a part of a mechanical system.

debris (duh-BREE): scattered pieces of something that has been wrecked or destroyed.

decommissioning (dee-kuh-MISH-uhn-ing): removing from active service.

deficiencies (dih-FISH-uhn-seez): things that people lack.

digital (DIJ-ih-til): relating to electronic forms or computers.

diodes (DAHY-ohds): a device, as a two-element electron tube or a semiconductor, through which current can pass freely in only one direction.

dissipate (DIS-uh-peyt): to scatter or disperse.

engineering (en-juh-NIHR-ing): the science of building machines or structures.

Ethernet (EE-ther-net): a system for connecting a number of computer systems to form a network.

fertilizer (FUR-tuh-lize-ur): a substance added to soil to make plants grow better.

helipad (HEL-uh-pad): a takeoff and landing area for helicopters.

high-definition (HAHY def-uh-NISH-uhn): a system for screen display of images that are sharper and more detailed than normal.

Kevlar (KEV-lahr): a kind of very strong fiber.

mimic (MIK-ik): to copy.

NASA (NAS-ah): the National Aeronautics and Space Administration; the government agency in charge of the U.S. space program.

orbits (OR-bits): the path of an object that is circling a planet or the Sun.

photovoltaic (foh-toh-vol-TEY-ik): relating to the production of an electric current using things exposed to light.

propulsion (pruh-PUHL-shuhn): the act of driving or pushing forward.

radiation (ray-dee-AY-shuhn): a kind of powerful energy made from high-energy particles.

resistance (ri-ZISS-tuhnss): the slowing or stopping effect of one thing on another.

rovers (ROH-verz): vehicles used to explore the surfaces of planets or other solid surfaces in space.

satellites (SAT-uh-lites): spacecraft that are sent into outer space to gather and send back information.

semiconductor (sem-ee-kuhn-DUHK-ter): a crystal material, such as silicon, that can conduct electricity.

spectrum (SPEK-trum): an array of light.

thermal (THUR-muhl): made to hold in heat.

truss (TRUHS): a triangular-shaped structural frame.

ultrasound (UHL-truh-sound): sound with a frequency greater than 20,000 Hz, approximately the upper limit of human hearing.

Wi-Fi (WAHY-fahy): a network that allows computers or smartphones to connect to the internet or communicate wirelessly.

zero gravity (GRAV-uh-tee): the state when there is no apparent gravity, the force that pulls things toward each other.

FOR MORE INFORMATION

Books
Aguilar, David A. *Space Encyclopedia*. Washington, DC: National Geographic, 2020.
Tour the solar system and beyond in this comprehensive book on space exploration.

Anderson, Amy, and Brian Anderson. *Space Dictionary for Kids*. New York, NY: Routledge, 2016.
Learn all about rockets, astronauts, the universe, and the fascinating world of space exploration.

DeGrasse Tyson, Neil. *Astrophysics for Young People in a Hurry*. New York, NY: Norton Young Readers, 2019.
Read about the mysteries of the universe in this accessible and exciting book.

Koontz, Robin. *Our Place in Space*. Vero Beach, FL: Rourke Educational Media, 2016.
Explore Earth's place in the universe and learn space-related facts.

Websites
NASA Kids' Club (https://www.nasa.gov/kidsclub/index.html)
NASA provides an online place for children to play as they learn about NASA and its missions.

NASA Science Space Place (https://spaceplace.nasa.gov)
NASA's award-winning Space Place website engages children in space and Earth science through interactive games, hands-on activities, and more.

National Geographic Kids—Facts About Mars (https://www.natgeokids.com/uk/discover/science/space/facts-about-mars/)
Young readers will uncover cool facts about the Red Planet.

National Geographic Kids—History of Space Travel (https://kids.nationalgeographic.com/space/article/history-of-space-travel)
Learn about the history of humans traveling into space.

Space Center Houston (https://spacecenter.org/exhibits-and-experiences/journey-to-space/)
Space Center Houston is a leading science and space exploration learning center.

Places to Visit

Kennedy Space Center in Merritt Island, FL (https://www.kennedyspacecenter.com/?utm_source=google&utm_medium=yext)
NASA's Kennedy Space Center features exhibits and historic spacecraft and memorabilia.

The National Air and Space Museum in Washington, DC (https://www.si.edu/museums/air-and-space-museum)
The National Air and Space Museum maintains the world's largest and most significant collection of aviation and space artifacts.

Rose Center for Earth and Space in New York, NY (https://www.amnh.org/exhibitions/permanent/rose-center)
Explore the cosmos, the history of the universe, galaxies, Earth, and more at the Rose Center at the American Museum for Natural History.

INDEX

Advanced Plant Habitat (APH), 27
Axiom Space, 38-39
Blue Origin, 38
Canadarm2 (robotic arm), 18
CEVIS (Cycle Ergometer with Vibration Isolation System), 23
Currie, Nancy, 11
Dextre, 18
Earth, 5-8, 12, 15, 17, 19-20, 25, 27, 30, 32, 34, 36, 41-43
Ethernet cables, 31
exercise, 22-23
flight control teams, 19
flowers, 25
Glover, Victor, 4, 6, 20-21, 23, 28, 42-43
gravity, 7, 22
Gulf of Mexico, 42
health, 19, 24-25, 34-35
Hopkins, Mike, 4, 6, 20, 28, 30-31, 42
insulation, 17
International Space Station (ISS),
  building, 10-12, 14
  cupola, 17, 25, 38
  decommissioning of, 36
  exterior, 14
  future work, 36-43
  living on, 12-13, 20-35
  new stations, 38
  sleeping on, 32
  toilets on, 33
Japanese Space Agency (JAXA), 4
Johnson Space Center, 19
Kelly, Scott, 25
Kevlar, 17
laboratory experiments, 24-27
laser communications, 41
LED (light emitting diodes) lights, 26
Mars, 41
Meir, Jessica, 33
microgravity, 7, 20, 22-24, 35
Mission Control Centers, 19, 30
Musk, Elon, 5
NASA, 4, 6, 11, 15-16, 20, 33, 36, 38-39, 41
Noguchi, Soichi, 4, 42
photovoltaic cells, 15
plants, 24, 26-27
Point Nemo, 36
propulsion systems, 41
Quest airlock, 28
recovery ship, 42
return journey, 43
robotic arm, 11, 18-19
rovers, 41
Russia, 10, 12
semiconductor, 15
Sierra Space, 38
solar arrays, 14-16
space junk, 36
spacesuits, 24, 29, 41
spacewalks, 28-31
SpaceX, 4-5, 8, 43
thermal radiators, 16
truss structure, 14, 16
Ungar, Gene, 16
United States, 10-11
Unity module, 11
Vegetable Production System (Veggie), 26-27
vegetables, 24-27
vital signs, 32, 34
vitamin deficiencies, 24
Walker, Shannon, 4, 20, 22, 24, 42
water recycling, 33
Wi-Fi network, 31
Zarya module, 10-11
zero gravity (Zero-G), 6
Zvezda module, 12

ABOUT THE AUTHOR

Joyce Markovics has written hundreds of books for kids. She lives in an old house along the Hudson River. She is fascinated by space and all the things we still don't know about the universe. She would like to extend a Jupiter-sized thank you to Dr. Joel Green for partnering with her on this book series.